S0-EKK-369

A Recollection of
MARCELLA SEMBRICH

A Recollection of

MARCELLA SEMBRICH

H. GODDARD OWEN

New introduction by
PHILIP LIESON MILLER

CONECO LITHO GRAPHICS • GLENS FALLS, NY • 1995

Library of Congress Cataloging in Publication Data

Owen, H. Goddard, d. 1978
  A recollection of Marcella Sembrich.

  Reprint of the 1950 edition published by The Marcella
Sembrich Memorial Association.
    1. Sembrich, Marcella, 1858-1935. 2. Singers — United
States — Biography. I. Title.
ML420.S47093   1982   782.1'092'4   [B]   81-22197
ISBN 0-306-76141-6   AACR2

This 1995 reprint edition of *A Recollection of Marcella Sembrich* is an unabridged republication of the first edition published in New York in 1950. It is reprinted by arrangement with The Marcella Sembrich Memorial Association, Inc.

Copyright 1950 by The Marcella Sembrich Memorial Association, Inc.
Introduction copyright © 1981 by Philip Lieson Miller

Printed by Coneco Litho Graphics
58 Dix Avenue, Glens Falls, NY 12801

All Right Reserved

Manufactured in the United States of America

INTRODUCTION

IT HAS often been said that great voices and great musician-ship do not come in the same singers. If there is some truth in this, Marcella Sembrich is a brilliant exception. Her voice, from all accounts, was of unmatched purity and limpidity, capable of the most dazzling feats of coloratura, yet essentially a lyric, expressive voice. As Henry E. Krehbiel wrote after her New York debut in 1883, "It awakens memories of Mme. Patti's organ, but has a warmer lifeblood in it." But Sembrich was one of the finest musicians of her day, a friend and colleague of such masters as Paderewski, Kreisler, and the Flonzaley Quartet, with whom she enjoyed playing chamber music. Before she decided to make her career as a singer she had perfected her technique both as violinist and pianist.

Yet for all its refinement and musicianship, her art could never be called *caviare to the general*. The public adored her while the critics praised her. In addition to her musical gifts she had her full share of personal charms. She was adjudged an ex-cellent actress, an irresistible comedienne. And never has a great singer been so beloved by her colleagues. When she said good-bye to the opera in 1909, after a career of 31 years, her gala was an occasion still unmatched in the annals of the Metropolitan. And when she died in 1935, St. Patrick's Cathedral was full to overflow—a scene described by Marcia Davenport in her fictional prima donna's story, *Of Lena Geyer.*

After her retirement from the opera Mme. Sembrich continued for several years her career as a recitalist. Though it is not quite accurate to credit her with the first lieder recitals in this country, she did provide a model in programming that was followed for many years. And increasingly she interested herself in folksongs, which became a feature of her recitals. She was planning a series of four historical programs for the season of 1916/17, but illness prevented her from giving more than one; 4 February 1917 was the date of her final appearance.

In the course of the next few years she found herself deeply involved in yet another career, that of a teacher. She was the first head of the vocal department both at the Juilliard School in New York and at the Curtis Institue in Philadelphia. She had already done some teaching. Queena Mario, who made her debut in 1919, was a Sembrich pupil, and Alma Gluck, already an established artist, had come to her to perfect her art. When Maria Jeritza burst upon the New York scene in 1921, amid public adulation, some critics pointed out certain vocal problems and recommended study with Sembrich, which advice was gratefully taken. The long list of other distinguished pupils includes the names of Dusolina Giannini, Hulda Lashanska, Anna Hamlin, Edith Piper, Winifred Cecil, Harriet Eells, Harriet Van Emden, Polyna Stoska, and Louise Lerch. For several summers she took a group of them to Lake Placid, where they could study under more relaxed conditions.

In 1922 she acquired a property at Bolton, now Bolton Landing, and on a point of land along the shore of Lake George she built a studio. Happily, through the efforts of her daughter-in-law, Juliette de Coppet Stengel, the studio was opened in 1937 as a museum, and to maintain it the Marcella Sembrich Memorial Association was founded in 1940 by Mrs. Stengel Harriet Eells, and Harry Goddard Owen. The studio may be visited every summer between the first of July and Labor Day. One is struck by the breadth of Mme. Sembrich's circle—mementos of innumerable great singers and musicians are to be seen here, a permanent exhibit of her period in opera—and the depth of her interests.

Sembrich's American career coincided with the early days of the Victrola, and she made a long list of recordings, Even earlier she had visited the studio of Colonel Bettini in New York, where the voices of many opera singers were caught on perishable cylinders; at least one of Sembrich's has survived (Johann Strauss's *Voci di Primavera* has been reproduced on a seven-inch disc for the benefit of the record archives at Stanford University). She was also one of the seven opera singers who made the first Grand Opera discs for the Columbia Company in 1903. But from 1904 to 1911 she was a Victor artist. Admittedly the records do her scant justice, for as Sembrich herself confessed, she was never comfortable in front of the big acoustic recording horn. Nevertheless, some of them are quite beautiful and others have lovely moments. In respect to the quality of the voice itself, some imagination is required, but as with all acoustic records, it is safe to say that if the voice sounds beautiful it was undoubtedly more so in real life.

It may seem remarkable that so universally acclaimed an artist and so beloved a personality has not attracted a professional biographer. She herself never took time to write her memoirs, as so many of her colleagues did (for better or for worse), but her career is thoroughly documented in the sheaves of programs and clippings she saved. They are now in the archives of the Association. Taken together they provide something of a history of opera in her time. But Sembrich's life was not material for a popular biography simply because her life was her career. She never indulged in the kind of capers by which so many prima donnas make headlines. In 1877 she married her piano teacher, Wilhelm Stengel, 14 years her senior, and until his death in 1917 they were a devoted couple.

This appreciation by Harry Goddard Owen gives the outline of her life story with warmth and affection. If there is a questionable fact or two, this may be taken to show that Sembrich did leave some legends. There is a story on page 17 about her playing for Liszt. Henry E. Krehbiel, in an article published in the New York Herald-Tribune after Sembrich's death, tells the same story but as an audition with Julius Epstein whose advice was sought on whether she should play for Liszt. Krehbiel's authority was Professor Stengel. But the advice, ". . . sing, sing for the world, for you have the voice of an angel," is generally credited to Liszt.

Henry Goddard Owen was a man of broad interests and an important educator in the fine arts. An amateur pianist, he was especially interested in music. Born in Port Henry, N.Y. in 1902, he was educated at Middlebury College and Columbia University, where he took his master's degree. He taught at New York University and at Middlebury, where he was assistant professor of English. After service in the Navy in World War II, he was appointed dean of the college of arts and sciences at Rutgers in 1948, and later served as dean of the university for graduate work. He retired in 1965 and died on 20 April 1978.

PHILIP LIESON MILLER
New York City
October 1981

A Recollection of
MARCELLA SEMBRICH

A Recollection of

MARCELLA SEMBRICH

H. GODDARD OWEN

Dean, College of Arts and Sciences
Rutgers University

THE MARCELLA SEMBRICH MEMORIAL ASSOCIATION

In this sketch of her life, the lines in quotation marks relating to the girlhood of Marcella Sembrich were in part drawn from magazine articles which appeared in Poland during 1935 — the year of Mme. Sembrich's passing.

Other material has been gathered from the wealth of articles written both in America and in Europe largely during her lifetime.

Copyright, 1950

By

THE MARCELLA SEMBRICH MEMORIAL ASSOCIATION, INC.

All Rights Reserved — no part of this book may be reprinted in any form without permission in writing from the Association.

Printed in the U.S.A. by the

TRIGGS COLOR PRINTING CORPORATION

NEW YORK

A Recollection of

MARCELLA SEMBRICH

IN THE CITY OF ATHENS
which exerted such profound influence upon the arts
COMMENCED A CAREER
which was in its way to provide a standard
OF SUPREME ACHIEVEMENT

MARCELLA SEMBRICH
1858-1935

AN EARLY LIKENESS

"So be we true to ourselves nothing shall take from us
the reverence for lofty ideals of beauty"...

Earliest Home of Marcella Sembrich (née Kochanska)

MARCELLA SEMBRICH'S career was international as to her artistry and achievements, but peculiarly American as to what the new world gave to her, and what she gave to the new world. She was brought here in her early twenties, already famous, as part of the most brilliant array of talent the world of opera has ever known, at the period when grand opera was to be given permanent establishment in New York City. The renown which she and her fellow artists brought to the Metropolitan Opera Company came back to her and to them in fullest echo during what history now calls the "Golden Age of Song".

The peculiar nature of her gifts, the length and comprehensiveness of her career, above all the integrity of her standards and the thoroughness of her workmanship made her contribution to America's musical development incomparably rich, far-reaching and definitive.

A RECOLLECTION OF MARCELLA SEMBRICH

PRAXEDE MARCELLINE KOCHANSKA, whom the world was to know as Marcella Sembrich, was born in extreme poverty of humble Polish stock in a hamlet near Lemberg on February 15, 1858. Both her parents were musical. Her father's family had been tanners by trade for generations back. He, however, in his boyhood felt irresistibly drawn to music. He did not hesitate to forsake his family and native village for some distant town where his dream could come true of joining an itinerant military band, and where he could realize his long-suppressed desire to learn every musical instrument. Although by profession a violinist, he became a village organist besides. In later years, seeking to discover new fields for his own teaching of music, Casimir Kochanski while exploring the neighboring districts journeyed with his little family in a country wagon with their belongings piled about them. And thus the tiny Marcella, securely banked in a hollow of hay, began to travel before she began to walk. In earliest childhood her companions were sunny meadows, rippling brooks and the wonders of the sky.

At a tender age Marcella was brought by her parents to the country town of Bolechow, south of Lemberg, where she spent part of her childhood, with a disciplined background provided by her father's severity. Here their modest dwelling was built by Casimir Kochanski, whose inventive skill enabled him to construct almost anything from musical instruments to a home for his family.

When Casimir began Marcella's musical education, he

seated her at the piano at the age of four, improvising an arrangement whereby she might reach the pedals. When she was six, he gave her her first lessons on the violin that he had made for her, so ardent was his desire to impart his knowledge to his most gifted child. In this way, musical instruments became her toys long before they became her tools. Especially from her father, Marcella inherited her pronounced love of study and untiring application. In appearance, however, she more nearly resembled her mother, who was born in Cracow. Juliana Sembrich Kochanska was clever and industrious, — a woman full of tolerance and a devoted parent in the face of her family's hardships.

When but a child, Marcella was entrusted with attending to the family laundering in a nearby stream, a duty which she regarded as pure fun, in contrast to hours of unbroken concentration in the daily life of her over-studious childhood.

Owing to their scanty means, Marcella still a little girl, was obliged to make copies of borrowed scores for quartette playing in the humble Kochanski home, for it was natural for all members of the family to take part in ensembles, — her mother and brother playing violin, her father cello, with Marcella at the piano. The arduous task of copying their respective parts she often accomplished by candlelight; this permanently impaired Marcella's eyesight, so that during her career she could scarcely see the conductor's baton; yet later, and even in her advanced age, this handicap never deterred her in her study of an entirely new repertory of vocal music with which the new tides of the twentieth century supplemented the classics of her youth.

At the age of ten the first significant opportunity was given Marcella to play in public. In later years she wrote, "That happy event stands out in my memory as though it were but yesterday." To further her natural gifts, Marcella when eleven years old was brought to the Conservatory of Lemberg through the influence of a gallant old villager whom the children knew as "Granddaddy Janowicz". On her way, accompanied by her father, she carried her music rolled up in a red handkerchief. At the Conservatory Marcella majored in violin under Bruckmann and entered the piano class of Professor Stengel, who was also of Polish birth and a pupil of Moscheles.

The Director of the Conservatory was Charles Mikuli, recognized as Chopin's best pupil. "Upon hearing the gifted Marcella, compassion aroused by her threadbare appearance soon gave way to admiration. Mikuli was so struck by the talent of the amazing Kochanska, still so young, that he himself became her instructor in harmony. Her appreciation, gentleness, obedience and natural sense of humor won the hearts of old and young alike." "It now became Professor Stengel's inspired task to introduce her to the wonderland of music — Bach, Beethoven, Chopin — and to watch over her artistic development." "The fact that she began her musical education at the Lemberg Conservatory became that institution's greatest glory". . . .

Snow-covered roofs of Lemberg
the Capital of Galicia

Above – Identified as the house where Marcella occupied the hall bedroom during her musical studies in Lemberg

During these years of study "Marcella met her expenses by playing the piano for children's dancing classes, and she was also the expert provider of spirited mazurkas and rhythmic waltzes at night-long parties of the élite. Marcella was then slim, small and dark, with sparkling brown eyes and an enchanting smile that remained unchanged all her life." "Little did the shy Marcella suspect that before ten years would elapse, the foremost operatic centers would be disputing the right to claim her." In 1873, when plans were in progress for her further study in Vienna, she gave a concert before leaving Lemberg, alternately playing the piano and the violin, in the spacious Starbek Hall, now a moving picture auditorium. Probably Professor Stengel suspected at the time that she also had a voice.

When finally Marcella arrived in Vienna, that enchanting city of music, she soon was studying piano with Epstein, violin with Helmesberger, and began her voice-study with Rokitansky — names which stand through the years as those of great teachers. "It will ever be to the credit of Professor Stengel that he made possible this period of study in Vienna, for it formed the basis of that broad musical culture which lay at the very root of her artisic being."

"For her first interview with Julius Epstein, Marcella prepared Beethoven's piano Sonata in E Minor, Etudes of Moschelès and Preludes and Inventions of Bach." "When she played the violin for Helmesberger, he declared her pronounced talent so outstanding that she almost made the decision of devoting herself exclusively to that instrument."

Liszt's home in Weimar

Marcella is heard by Franz Liszt — 1875

While pursuing her studies "Marcella was in a very serious mood, busy with her own thoughts and her work; she declined all invitations and made the most unheard-of progress in her singing." "When the year was over", she later remarked, "it was clear to me which path I longed to pursue, for I realized that with my voice I could express more eloquently my reverence for the art that filled my soul." To a friend of her childhood Marcella writes: "Professor Schell, who takes great interest in me, wants me to meet Liszt when he comes. He wants me to sing and play for him. They say I can reach great achievement — but enough of that — — what news of your garden?"

The following briefly gives the account of Marcella's playing for Liszt — that towering figure of his age:

"When she played for him, Liszt took the greatest interest in the little Marcelline Kochanska (Sembrich). The old master, kindly in expression, yet never without that inimitably sarcastic smile hovering faintly about the corners of his mouth, asked the young Slavic maiden to play something. She modestly asked:

"Bach or Beethoven, master, — Schumann or Chopin?"

Liszt shook his shaggy locks and laughed:

"It seems you have a repertoire?" he queried, and Marcelline in demure accents answered:

"Perhaps some Liszt?", and, without waiting for a reply, she went to the grand piano, seated herself, and placing her feet on the pedals, dashed into the pompous introduction of the master's twelfth Hungarian Rhapsody. The boldness of her attack, the surety of her fingers and her fire and freedom pleased the great pianist exceedingly. When she had finished, he asked in a bantering manner:

"What else?" She took out her violin, and plucking its strings a moment to test the tuning of the instrument, she began one of Wieniawski's Polish melodies, and soon demonstrated her excellent bowing and rich *cantabile*.

"Anything else, young lady?" Liszt asked. Her answer to this was to sing for him. She sang like a lark, and Liszt burst into enthusiastic applause.

"My little angel", he said in German, "God has given you three pairs of wings with which to fly through the country of music; they are all equal: give up none of them, but sing, sing for the world, for you have the voice of an angel."

This generous praise and sensitive counsel echoed Marcella's own conviction that singing was the art to which she was to devote her life. Accordingly, in 1875, accompanied by her mother, she went to Milan for eight months of study under G. Lamperti. There while learning Italian, she also continued with piano and violin. In 1876-77 she was to have a second period of study with Francesco Lamperti, of whom Sembrich spoke in later life as her only teacher. "His remarkable technical knowledge, power of expression and stupendous enthusiasm were to her an inexhaustible source of inspiration."

12 Via Ospedale — Milan
where Marcella lived with her mother

Milan – 1877 – Student days with Francesco Lamperti

"While in Milan, Marcella continued to live very simply, entirely for her art." She had a voice of wide range, extreme clarity and resonance, with a brilliantly expressive upper register. "What most distinguished her singing was her wonderful ability for sustained melody, her command of breath and a musical comprehension absolutely beyond reproach. Being especially gifted linguistically and immensely quick-minded, she learned with great facility." Without knowing it, Marcella herself described her voice in terms which explain the unique position she was to occupy in the operatic world in later years. "My voice develops a great deal", she wrote a friend in Poland, "It is coloratura, but more a dramatic coloratura." It was a voice suited to her temperament, but it is interesting that even in her girlhood she realized something of the rare nature of her vocal inclination. A "dramatic coloratura" is quite unusual in itself, and this Sembrich truly had; but she had also an innate musical endowment, and she developed a mastery of interpretation which was to bring her preëminence in the altogether different field of lieder-singing.

On June 3, 1877, at the age of nineteen, she made her operatic début in Athens. Of two offers which she received while a young student, she chose to accept the one that would take her to the Capital of Greece, because of happy expectations of an enchanting journey by boat. She always remembered that first performance in the open-air theatre before King George I and his court under starlit skies with the Acropolis shimmering in the distance.

PROFESSOR GUILLAUME STENGEL

At the time of filling this first engagement, Marcella made the momentous decision of entrusting her life's happiness in marriage to Professor Stengel, who had loved her since her childhood.

As 'Dinorah'
(From a later photograph)

In Athens she had been engaged to sing twenty-four performances of 'I Puritani', 'Lucia di Lammermoor' and 'Dinorah' and as she came again and again before the footlights to bow her thanks to the audience, intimations were evident of an assured future for the youthful singer.

With a wisdom that characterized her throughout her life, she determined upon further study and returned to Vienna, where she perfected her repertory in the German language under the coach, Richard Lewy, while studying the dramatic interpretations of her roles with the actress, Marie Seebach. "She continued constantly to improve her dramatic and vocal technique." At this time Marcella adopted her mother's maiden name of Sembrich for her professional career.

In the Spring of 1878 she was engaged for the Saxon Royal Opera in Dresden, and during her stay there, Marcella received an occasional leave of absence when she availed herself of opportunities to appear in opera in Milan, Vienna or Warsaw.

It was on New Year's Day in 1879, at the Leipzig Gewandhaus, that Brahms conducted the first performance of his violin concerto, dedicated to and played by Joseph Joachim, the most eminent violinist of his day. On this impressive occasion the vocal artist was none other than the youthful Marcella Sembrich.

ELEVENTH
SUBSCRIPTION CONCERT
IN THE HALL "GEWANDHAUS" IN LEIPZIG
Wednesday, Jan. 1st, 1879

PART I

Overture suite .... Franz Lachner

Aria from "DIE ENTFÜHRUNG" ...... Mozart
    sung by Marcella Sembrich

Concerto for violin ...... Joh. Brahms
    played by Joseph Joachim
(The composer will conduct his new manuscript)

Lieder ..... sung by Marcella Sembrich

Chaconne for violin .... Bach
    played by Joseph Joachim

PART II

Symphony Nº 7 ..... Ludwig von Beethoven

ABONNEMENT-CONCERT

im Saale des Gewandhauses zu Leipzig

Mittwoch, den 1. Januar 1879.

— · — · · —

Erster Theil.

Ouverture (aus der Suite Nr. IV) von Franz Lachner.

Arie aus der Oper: „Die Entführung aus dem Serail" von W. A. Mozart, gesungen von Fräulein *Marcella Sembrich*, Königl. Sächs. Hofopernsängerin aus Dresden.

> Martern aller Arten
> Mögen meiner warten,
> Ich verlache all' dein Droh'n!
> Nichts soll mich erschüttern,
> Dann nur würd' ich zittern,
> Könnt ich untreu jemals sein.
>
> Lass dich bewegen!
> Verschone mich!
> Des Himmels Segen
> Belohne dich!
>
> Doch dich rührt kein Flehen,
> Standhaft, sollst du sehen,
> Duld' ich jede Qual und Noth.
> Ordne nur, gebiete,
> Drohe, strafe, wüthe,
> Zuletzt befreit mich doch der Tod.

Concert für die Violine von Joh. Brahms (neu, Manuscript, unter Leitung des Componisten), vorgetragen von Herrn *Joseph Joachim*.

Program — January 1, 1879

Interior of the historic Gewandhaus — in Leipzig

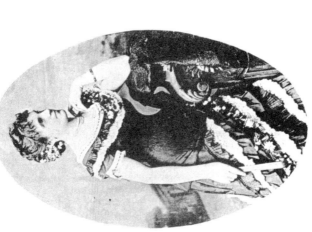

On January 1, 1879 these artists were heard at the Gewandhaus

Joachim   Sembrich   Brahms

5 humorous poses of Johannes Brahms

Collection of Madame Sembrich

Early in the Spring of 1880, at one of the famous Lower Rhine Festivals, she was heard again, and reports of her extraordinary success soon reached England. When Marcella's intention to go to London became known in Dresden, the news brought consternation to all music lovers, for they had discovered for themselves that a new star had dawned. From orchestra and audience came a memorial token bearing the message, "Stay here — Stay with us."

Program 2-go Koncertu

Sala Aleksandryjska w Ratuszu.

W Poniedziałek, dnia 21 Kwietnia (3 Maja 1880) roku,
o godzinie 8-mej wieczorem.

Program 2-go Koncertu

Pani MARCELINY

SEMBRICH-KOCHAŃSKIEJ

Nadwornej Królewsko-Saskiej Primadony.

w współudziałem:

PP. Michałowskiego, Górskiego i Paderewskiego.

1. **Arja z op. „Wolny Strzelec"**		K. M. Web-r
pani Sembrich-Kochańska		
2. **Polonez** As-dur.		Chopin.
p. Michałowski		
3. a. **Pieśń**		Fr. Ries.
b. **Kołysanka**		Taubert.
c. **Pieśń**		Förster.
d. **Ich wandre nicht**		Schumann.
pani Sembrich-Kochańska.		
4. a. **Romance**		Zarzycki.
b. **Polonez**		H. Wieniawski.
p. Górski.		
5. **Arja i sce z „Lunatyczki"**		Bellini
pani Sembrich-Kochańska.		
6. **Menuet**		Moszkowski.
Etude		Liszt
p. Michałowski.		
7. a. **Pieśń litewska**		Chopin.
b. **Znasz li ten kraj?**		Moniuszko.
c. „Piaszku luby, skowroneczku"		L. Grossman.
mazurek		
wykona pani Sembrich-Kochańska		
8. **Dwa mazurki**		H. Wieniawski
p. Górski.		
9. **Arja z op. „Flet zaczarowany"**		Mozart
pani Sembrich-Kochańska.		

Fortepian BECHSTEINA ze składu pp. Herman i Grossmann.

W drukarni Jana Cotty, ulica Daniłowiczowska N. 619. w Warszawie.

Sala Aleksandryjska w Ratuszu.

We Wtorek, dnia 15/27 Kwietnia 1880 r. o godzinie 8-mej wieczorem.

Program 1-go Koncertu

Pani MARCELINY

SEMBRICH-KOCHAŃSKIEJ

Nadwornej Królewsko-Saskiej Primadony.

Ze współudziałem: PP. Aleksandra Zarzyckiego, Dyrektora Warszawskiego Instytutu Muzycznego, Władysława Górskiego Józefa Gochwila i Ign. Paderewskiego.

1. **Trio**		Raff
wyk. pp. Zarzycki, Górski i Gochwil		
2. **Arja z Purytanów**		Bellini.
wyk. pani Sembrich-Kochańska.		
3. a. **Danse espagnol**		Moszkowski-Souret
b. **Menueto**		Mozart.
wyk. p. Górski.		
4. **Trzy pieśni**		L. Hartmann
a. Ich wandle...		
b. ...		
c. ...		
wyk. pani Sembrich-Kochańska.		
5. a. **Melancolie**		Rubinstein.
b. **Mazurek**		Zarzycki.
wyk. p. Zarzycki.		
6. **Trzy pieśni**		A. Zarzycki.
a. ...		
b. ...		
c. ...		
wyk. pani Sembrich-Kochańska.		
7. a. **Pieśń bez słów**		Górski
b. **Zingarella**		Górski
wyk. p. Górski.		
8. **Walc z opera z op. „Dinorah"**		Meyerbeer.
wyk. pani Sembrich-Kochańska.		

Fortepian BECHSTEINA ze składu pp HERMAN i GROSMAN

W drukarni Jana Cotty, ulica Daniłowiczowska N. 619. w Warszawie.

While in Warsaw in 1880, two concerts were given by Marcella Sembrich
Kochanska at which Ignace Paderewski played her accompaniments

ADELINA PATTI

BUCKINGHAM PALACE.

WEDNESDAY EVENING, 29th JUNE, 1881.

OVERTURE, "*A Midsummer's Night's Dream*" . . . . Mendelssohn.

NOTTURNO, "*Tornami a dir*," . . . . . . (Don Pasquale) Donizetti.
 Mad^e Sembrich & Sig^r Mancio.

ROMANZA, "*Quando le sere*," . . . . . (Luisa Miller) Verdi.
 Sig^r Nicolini.

BARCAROLLE, "*Les Contes d'Hoffmann*," . . . . . . Offenbach.
 Mad^e Adelina Patti & Patey, with Chorus.

CHORUS, "*Hymn to Bacchus*," . . . . . (Antigone) Mendelssohn.

CANZONE, "*Voi che sapete*," . . . (Le Nozze di Figaro) Mozart.
 Mad^e Adelina Patti.

ROMANZA, "*Spirto gentil*," . . . . (La Favorita) Donizetti.
 Sig^r Mancio.

SOLO & CHORUS, "*The Water Nymph*," . . . . . . Rubinstein.
 Mad^e Patey.

ARIA, "*Che far senza*," . . . . (Il Seraglio) Mozart.
 Mad^e Sembrich.

SCENA, ... (Mireille) Gounod.
 Mad^e Adelina Patti, Sig^r Nicolini & Del Puente, & Chorus.

CANZONE DEL TOREADOR, ... (Carmen) Bizet.
 Sig^r Del Puente.

QUARTETTO, "*Un dì, se ben rammentomi*," . . . (Rigoletto) Verdi.
 Mad^e Sembrich & Patey, Sig^r Mancio & Del Puente.

God Save the Queen.

Conductor, ... Mr. W. G. Cusins.

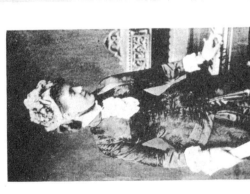

MARCELLA SEMBRICH

Program of a Command Performance at Buckingham Palace
where Marcella appeared with Adelina Patti – 1881

Adelina Patti in Ricci's 'Crispina e la Comare'

Marcella's first visit to London occurred in May 1880. Her audition came about when the young vocal artist and her husband arrived at Covent Garden as Adelina Patti was finishing a rehearsal. The sceptical impresario, Ernest Gye, was in no mood to be delayed by listening to a newcomer. But the insistence of the conductor prevailed upon him to grant Marcella the audition. Then, in the deserted auditorium, the girl of twenty-two with the dark burning eyes and the delicate, sensitive mouth, let soar the voice whose fame was later to sweep around the planet. It rose and fell across the half-lit stage, resounding in the brilliant and poignant accents of Donizetti's arias from 'Lucia di Lammermoor', which brought Marcella an immediate engagement for five successive years. The tired orchestra which for her sake had been detained, rose in a body to applaud her. With her contract in hand, she was off on her spectacularly successful London engagement. She captured the critics, one of whom wrote: "It is long since any singer has appeared who could challenge a comparison with her greatest predecessors."

There and then, too, she met her idol of student days, Adelina Patti, with whom she appeared in 1881 at a command performance at Buckingham Palace. Marcella's enthusiasm for Patti had first been kindled six years earlier upon hearing her at the magnificent Opera House in Vienna.

Triumph followed triumph for Marcella when she was heard in Madrid, Lisbon, Warsaw, Russia and France. "Genius was in her. From the time she was a little girl it was as plain and compelling as her candor."

Marcella Sembrich
in the Spring of 1879

. . . and a few years later

Nordica

Sembrich

Concert program, season of 1880-81, when Nordica and Sembrich were heard on the same program during their first visit at St. Petersburg. Lillian Nordica's artistic achievements of later years are remembered as among the finest of America's many contributions to the lyric stage.

A RECOLLECTION OF MARCELLA SEMBRICH

Her first appearance in opera at St. Petersburg and in Moscow coincided with Lillian Nordica's engagement in 1880-81 at the Imperial Opera at St. Petersburg, where the young American soprano won her audience with her magnificent voice, handsome presence and delightful personality. The two youthful artists thus brought together at the start of their careers, were heard in concert on the same program. In those early seasons at St. Petersburg, one of the youngest members of the opera orchestra was the distinguished Serge Koussevitsky.

Occasionally on concert programs Sembrich included Polish songs, one of which in particular aroused outbursts of patriotic fervor among her fellow-countrymen in what was at that time Russian Poland.

While at St. Petersburg Sembrich sang for Czar Alexander II and his family in the Winter Palace. At the conclusion of the evening the Czar said: "But there is a little song for which you are famous. Will you not sing it?" "I think", came the reply, "Your Majesty speaks of the Chopin song that I sing only in Polish, and therefore your Chief of Police has given emphatic instructions not to sing it again." The Czar smiled, "But I should like to hear it," he repeated. Thereupon, seating herself at the piano, Sembrich sang in Polish for the ruler of her oppressed country the song which poignantly expressed the joy and sorrow of her people. "You have moved me greatly", said the Czar, "and I shall not forget Poland." "Subsequently he bestowed upon her a simple gold bracelet set with seven diamonds, which Sembrich frequently wore as a talisman.

As Zerlina in 'Don Giovanni' by Mozart

In the midst of her youthful triumphs, already an assured prima donna in the leading European Opera Houses, Sembrich was brought to New York City for an event brilliant and controversial enough in its own day, but of an importance that has only magnified with ensuing years. That event was the founding of the Metropolitan Opera Company. At the time it was regarded merely as the opening of a new theatre of imposing design, intended to challenge, but not expected to surpass, the already established operatic stronghold in the city. Its location on what at that period was the upper edge of fashionable New York, was the first step in an operatic war that was to involve the leading artists of the day, and the whole of New York's social, theatrical, journalistic and financial worlds as well. The old Academy of Music was flourishing at Union Square. The new Opera House at 39th & Broadway, which was built as a rival, finally superseded and destroyed it. But at the outset the struggle promised to be equal, and rival companies of the world's most famous singers were assembled to vie with each other in that winter of 1883-84 when the Metropolitan Opera House offered its initial season. Under the direction of Henry E. Abbey, who had been certain enough of Sembrich to schedule her American début on the second night of the season, traditionally the riskiest evening of the year, Sembrich was first heard in the land she was later to adopt, in a performance of 'Lucia di Lammermoor' October 24, 1883. The performance was a triumph for Sembrich, and on that occasion Henry E. Krehbiel wrote of her singing:

"It united some of the highest elements of art which can be found only in one richly endowed with deep musical feeling and ripe artistic intelligence. She carried her voice wondrously well through a wide register, and from the lowest note to the highest there is the same quality. It awakens echoes of Mme. Patti's organ, but has a warmer lifeblood in it."

And from another paper we quote:
"Sembrich's voice has that unique quality which is the vocal equivalent of originality in literature and art."

And of her Amina in 'La Sonnambula':
"One is almost startled by hearing tones of a most pronounced dramatic quality."

During this first New York winter, Sembrich was on terms of warm friendship with Christine Nilsson, the established favorite of the public, who, with Italo Campanini, had lent extreme brilliance to the opening performance of the Metropolitan season in 'Faust'. This world-renowned prima donna and her rising young colleague enjoyed their brisk walks together on Sunday mornings in Central Park. Another of Sembrich's friends in this period was Patti herself, — their friendship having originated at the time of their joint appearance at Buckingham Palace. Crossing the Atlantic together, the two singers had their steamer chairs placed side by side, and when occasionally Adelina Patti hummed her cadenzas, she was astonished at the rapidity with which Marcella jotted them down.

As Amina in 'La Sonnambula', a role in which Marcella Sembrich was heard in 1883 during the opening season of the Metropolitan.

(The above photograph is of a later period)

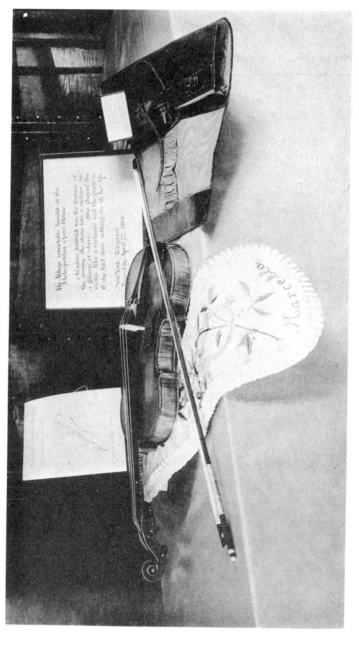

The day following the Abbey benefit at the Metropolitan, a New York paper stated; "Madame Sembrich was the feature of the evening. She shone like a meteor in a galaxy of stars. She played the violin like a virtuoso, and the piano as though she had done nothing else all her life."

(The above photograph shows the cover she made for the protection of her instrument.)

when everyone else is indulging.

Make sure that your pet does not have easy access to common Halloween decorations, such as burning candles, small costume pieces or accessories, and battery-operated decorations, all of which can pose burning, gas-

M.
doesn
ment
eyes.
dog
after
long
clear.

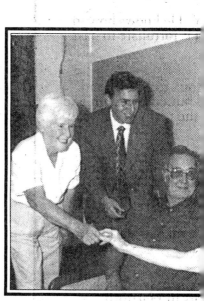

WE SUP
Fai

p. 43

read entire page:

"after that the house
went crazy .....
none of us who
were there have ever
forgotten the
impressions
of that night."

A RECOLLECTION OF MARCELLA SEMBRICH

During her first season in America, Sembrich made fifty-five appearances in eight of the leading cities, appearing in eleven of her roles. When the winter was over, she took part in a Spring concert given in Abbey's benefit in New York. Her scheduled share in this gala bill was a complete surprise to her ardent public. (Quoted from W. J. Henderson, who in 1930 recalled the event as follows):

"There was a plenty of curiosity just before the Gala Performance at the Metropolitan Opera House concluding the season of 1883-84. It had been announced that the brilliant Marcella Sembrich would play a violin solo. When she walked on the stage with her instrument, there were indulgent smiles and kindly applause. With the orchestra in the pit and Vianese in in the conductor's chair, Madame Sembrich with their support, standing alone on the stage, played the Adagio and Finale of the 7th Concerto of de Bériot. It did not take any of us long to realize that she was an accomplished violinist. The audience applauded and cheered when she finished. She was recalled eight or ten times, and finally sat down at the piano on the stage and played Chopin mazurkas, proving that she was an equally fine pianist. Then the audience went hysterical. Shouts and cheers until, after a dozen more recalls, she walked down to the footlights and spoke in a low tone to Vianese. He raised his baton and Madame Sembrich sang with unsurpassable beauty, Ah, non Giunge from 'La Sonnambula'. After that the house went crazy — but she had shown herself mistress of three executive branches of music and her feat was ended. None of us who were there have ever forgotten the impressions of that night."

And Krehbiel wrote:

> "In every instance Madame Sembrich was the complete artist,
> and the public who had been charmed by her witcheries as
> Mozart's Zerlina and melted by the pathos of her singing in
> the last act of 'La Traviata', was at a loss to say if she had
> shown herself a greater artist in song or in instrumental music,
> as pianist or violinist. It was not until many years after she
> had returned to Europe to continue her operatic triumphs
> that I learned the story of her life, and with it, the secret of
> her musical versatility. So far as I know, the story of Madame
> Sembrich is without a parallel."

Although she had carried off the artistic laurels of the season in 1883-84, Sembrich's career for more than a decade lay in Europe, where she now shared first honors with artists whose names were already great when as a little girl she was playing dance music at soirées in her native Lemberg. Her concert tours which had covered the foremost countries of Europe, were extended in 1886 to include Scandinavia and the Low Countries. In opera she became a world figure — acclaimed in the capitals of Europe. Her dynamic personality made her the idol of the public. Added to her extraordinary ability, was great histrionic talent. In her art, and particularly through the peculiarly stirring quality of a voice of superlative loveliness, lay the secret of the irresistible spell she exercised over her audience. "She had the almost unique ability to make a pianissimo as climactically impressive as a fortissimo — And what sheer ecstasy of unleashed tone and rhythm there was in a waltz song!" Dearer to her above all else was the depth of feeling that she inspired in human hearts throughout her life.

Of a Paris event James G. Huneker has written his impressions:

"Conceive my amazement when this modest-looking woman with the *spirituelle* face sat down before the piano, and, with a finger agility and a grace and delicacy that Joseffy would envy, played Chopin's E flat Polonaise. Then she tuned her violin, which was handed her by her husband, and dashed off Wieniawski's Polonaise in G, and in response to an overwhelming demand for an encore, gave the same composer's touching Legende. Then to further mystify us, Sembrich, with that enchanting smile of hers, sat once more at the piano and sang — ah, so divinely, Mme. Viardot-Garcia's transcription of Chopin's D major piano mazurka. When I got out in the open air I felt like throwing my hat up and crying aloud, 'A miracle, a miracle', — but I contented myself by buying all the Sembrich photographs I could find and boring my friends to death with —'Have you heard Sembrich? Have you seen her at the piano? Do you know that she fiddles like an angel?'. . .To divine Sembrich's versatility, her true depth of musical feeling, you must hear her after some flaming and brilliant Donizettean aria, sing Mozart's 'The Violet', or Schumann's 'Nussbaum'. She will bring tears to your eyes by her simplicity and 'innigkeit', — a great artist, and never so great as in simple music, for simplicity is the true test, the only touchstone of the great singer."

Evidently her appearance had been in a benefit performance, for only on such occasions was Mme. Sembrich heard in the three-fold capacity of singer, pianist and violinist.

Rosina of an early period — in "The Barber of Seville"
"What made her performance so electric and exciting was its facility,
its brilliance, and above all, its daring audacity."
First season of the Metropolitan Opera Company — 1883-84

In Paris the Théâtre du Châtelet was the accepted Opera House for visiting opera companies. With a seating capacity of over 3,000, it was the most suitable theatre for the presentation of great foreign celebrities. After Sembrich's performance of the Barber of Seville, one of the foremost French critics, Oscar Commetant, wrote in the Paris paper 'Le Figaro':

"God be praised. I am thirty years younger since Saturday night. Mme. Marcella Sembrich sang to me, it seemed as though she sang to me alone, so intently did I listen to her 'Rosina' in the 'Barbiere di Siviglia'. She was incomparable, — recalling the glorious time of our Théâtre when the greatest stars were shining. Ah, Madame, I am one of the oldest music critics of France, and come to tell you with the greatest sincerity, that in the whole of my life I never felt truer pleasure and deeper admiration than that which I experienced last night for your interpretation of 'Rosina'— a role in which you show such grace, originality, inspiration! You are a genuine wonder, — but you know all this by the enthusiastic receptions the public gave you so unanimously. . . . I will be called enthusiastic — and so I am about this divine angel of musical genius."

And from Henderson we have these lines:

"Technicalities cannot explain the magic of singing like hers. . . . But it is necessary to keep ever in mind that the voice alone could not have made Sembrich one of the immortals of song. Her most important equipment was her profoundly musical nature . . . her unfailing instinct for expression."

F A U S T.

Opera

SCORE USED BY GOUNOD
IN GOING OVER THE PART OF MARGUERITE
WITH MADAME SEMBRICH
HER INTERPRETATION BROUGHT FORTH
THIS EXCLAMATION FROM THE GREAT COMPOSER
"C'EST GRAND COMME UN PAGE!"

Gounod's lines in his score of 'Faust'—
"Here indeed is a rare Marguerite"

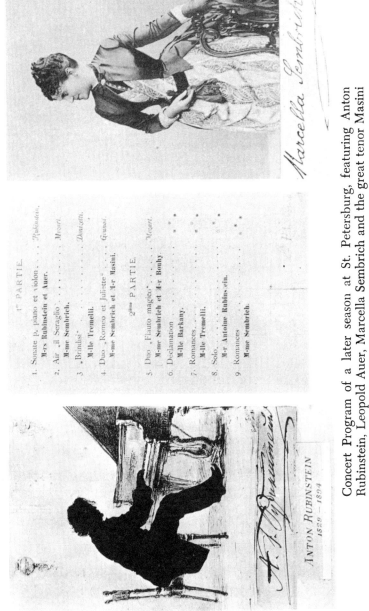

Concert Program of a later season at St. Petersburg, featuring Anton Rubinstein, Leopold Auer, Marcella Sembrich and the great tenor Masini

A RECOLLECTION OF MARCELLA SEMBRICH

It was in 1885 that Madame Sembrich first met Kitty · Wetmore, an American who resided entirely in Europe — a person of extraordinary culture. She was Madame Sembrich's close companion throughout all tours in foreign countries, and during summer holidays accompanied her on annual excursions in mountain climbing. This strong and lasting friendship endured through the years.

A concert tour in 1897 brought Madame Sembrich back to America, and for her appearance at the Metropolitan Opera House on October 26 her concert program included three of the great test pieces of soprano preëminence — Ah, non Giunge, Casta Diva from Bellini's 'Norma' and Martern Aller Arten from Mozart's 'Il Seraglio'. There was no season of opera at the Metropolitan that winter, but in the following autumn Sembrich again became a regular member of the Company.

In Spring Sembrich's operatic appearances continued on the European continent, but in winter they were mainly with the Metropolitan until her retirement from opera in 1909. It is a measure of her distinction that during these years it was she who kept the Italian repertoire alive and in high repute throughout New York's early fervid enthusiasm for Wagnerian music-drama.

"Although her voice forbade any attempt at heroic roles, she swept a marvelous gamut from joyous comedy through sentiment to the loftiest lyric poetry."

Marcella Sembrich is heard throughout Europe from 1884-1896

A performance of 'Romeo & Juliet' in Monte Carlo — 1893
with the three Polish artists —
Sembrich and the de Reszke brothers

Jean as 'Romeo'

Monte Carlo
and
Interior of theatre

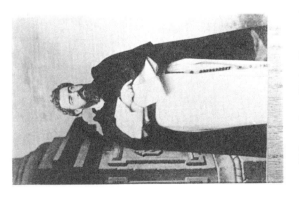

Edouard as 'Friar Laurent'

Her singing ever characterized by effortless technical mastery, was colored with a keen dramatic sense — but above all, she possessed that indescribable glowing magnetism, and that priceless gift called inspiration which belongs to genius.

Among her roles that of Violetta in 'La Traviata' was one of the public's favorites. Henderson once told Sembrich that her Violetta was the most moving he had seen on the stage. But she shook her head in grave protest, and with her usual freedom from all pretension, Sembrich chided him with: "Come now, you are very extravagant. Don't you remember Patti?" Sembrich was considered unsurpassable as Zerlina in 'Don Giovanni', as Susanna in 'Le Nozze di Figaro', as Queen of the Night in 'The Magic Flute', as Lucia di Lammermoor, as Rosina in 'Il Barbiere di Siviglia', as Marguerite in 'Faust', as Mimi in 'La Boheme'. Puccini said of her, "You are *the* Mimi". Curiously enough, — 'L'Elisir d'Amore' which later generations look upon as a tenor's opera, was an especially loved vehicle for Sembrich, and it was revived for her at the Metropolitan during her last seasons there. This will indicate to some extent the magic of her appeal and the sympathy of her impersonations. It was for her that the Metropolitan introduced the French version of Donizetti's 'La Fille du Régiment', as performed at the Paris Première. Earlier performances in New York had been given in Italian for Patti and Sonntag.

Sembrich's Wagnerian roles included Eva in 'Die Meister-singer' and Elsa in 'Lohengrin', so broad and secure was her flexible and vibrant voice. She had some thirty-seven roles at her command, sung in Italian, French and German, and as a European critic wrote as early as 1886, "Those who comprehend the great attributes revealed by this richly endowed woman know that coloratura singing is but a portion of that which constitutes her creative art."

All that was possible to crowd into a single performance turned Sembrich's farewell at the Metropolitan into what Krehbiel noted as 'an ovation, the like of which has probably no parallel in operatic history', and signified the departure of one of the most inspirational figures in the history of music in this country. The gala bill selected for this farewell in 1909 consisted of an act from Donizetti's 'Don Pasquale', the second act of Rossini's 'Il Barbiere di Siviglia' and the first act of Verdi's 'La Traviata', while the minor roles at the supper party were sung by such admirable artists as Scotti, Amato, Didur and Bada, and the ravishing Geraldine Farrar who showed particular honor to Sembrich by singing the small role of 'Flora'.

Interior of the Metropolitan in the days of Madame Sembrich
(Sketched during a performance)

Saturday Evening, Feb. 6, at 8 o'clock
Farewell Appearance in Opera
And Twenty-Fifth Anniversary of

MADAME SEMBRICH

DON PASQUALE--Act I

Norina	Mme. Sembrich
Dottore Malatesta	M. Scotti

Il Barbiere di Siviglia--Act II

Rosina	Mmes.	Sembrich
Berta		Mattfeld
Il Conte d'Almaviva	MM.	Bonci
Figaro		Campanari
Basilio		Didur
Dr Bartolo		Paterna
Un Ufficiale		Tecchi
Fiorello		Bégué

LA TRAVIATA--Act I

Violetta	Mmes.	Sembrich
Flora Bervoise		Farrar
Alfredo	MM.	Caruso
Barone Douphol		Scotti
Dottore Grenvil		Didur
Marchese d'Obigny		Amato
Gastone		Badà
Conductor	Mr. Francesco Spetrino	

Program of Farewell — 1909

As 'Norina' in Don Pasquale

Mme. Sembrich's illustrious colleagues, an assembly of brilliant stars including her friends, Emma Eames and Louise Homer, joined an adoring public, and united in paying tribute to an artist whose departure filled them with a sense of irreparable loss. Gifts were showered upon her — perhaps the most touching being the loving cup offered by the orchestra, and a handsome mirror from the chorus. From the Board of Directors who elected her an Honorary Member of the Metropolitan Company, she received a silver bowl, appropriately inscribed. A pearl necklace and watch and chain set in diamonds, purchased by public subscription, were presented to her by the Hon. Seth Low, Ex-Mayor of N. Y., who said:

> "Fare *you* well always and everywhere, fare *you* well: and let these pearls in their own beauty and in the beauty of the association through which they shine, say to you now and say to you always: 'Think not so much of the gift of the lovers as of the love of the givers'."

Then, amid unprecedented enthusiasm, Mme. Sembrich addressed the audience, telling them that she hoped they would keep a place for her in their hearts and memories. "Thus", again in the words of Krehbiel, "departed from the operatic stage one of the greatest stars that ever illumined it." As the gold curtains of the Metropolitan fell after the performance, they closed upon an unrivalled era.

"Admirable in dramatic spirit, the interest of the part rested upon Sembrich's acting and singing of 'Ulana', which part revealed her as a highly emotional singer."
(From the review of a New York paper in 1904 after a performance of the opera 'Manru' by Ignace Paderewski)

Sembrich and Caruso

in

'La Bohême' by Puccini

You are the Mimi —

"A voice quite as much at home in scenes of Mimi in 'La Bohême' as in the bravura of Astrafiammante in Mozart's 'Magic Flute'."—W. J. Henderson

And W. J. Henderson expressed a universal sentiment:

"Queen of the night, Queen of the singer's art,
Queen of the stage, Queen of the public heart!
    Hail and farewell! Your name is writ above,
Supreme in song, still more, supreme in love."

After her retirement from opera her career continued on the concert stage, and was devoted to the still subtler art of song. The period during which she established herself as a leading artist in the recital field coincided with the development of a discerning musical public in the United States, and her own position in the recital world was all the more fortified by the fact that other magnificent artists were including America in their itineraries and were finding here such acclaim as redoubled their European renown. Music in its finer aspects had attained a remarkable stage of advancement through the stimulus of dauntless pioneers, who had awakened in the American public a desire for a more profound knowledge of music.

Among those pioneers the Kneisel String Quartette brought only chamber music of the highest quality to the American cities it visited — a courageous practice in a period when concessions were universally being made to popular taste — the more so when one considers that chamber music is primarily an artform for connoisseurs. In the personality of Edward J. de Coppet the cause of chamber music found a patron of exalted devotion to music. He founded the Flonzaley String Quartette, which by its extensive yearly concert tours during a quarter of a century, added strong impetus to the growth of America's musical education.

Another great factor in this development was the conductor, Theodore Thomas, highly regarded in New York, and watched with interest as he established his own orchestra in Chicago. Thomas was a master of persuasion. He placed the unfamiliar and therefore unliked "new" music of Wagner at the close of his programs, so that those unwilling to hear it, might leave if they chose. And Sembrich, engaged to appear with him, was amazed that he asked her to sing so slight a ballad as "Some Day". Her standards were too high for her to understand at once the request for this number at a symphony concert, for Sembrich was the first of the great operatic sopranos to give in America what we know today as a recital program — a program not interspersed with operatic arias, but carefully chosen from the song repertory alone.

Her first New York concert, in March 1900, was a memorable one, for it set a fashion which has prevailed ever since.

When she first appeared in London, she had braved the tradition that divas in concert should confine themselves to operatic excerpts, and had sung German lieder. She startled New York by singing programs which included French and Italian songs of the 19th Century, together with music of Schubert, Schumann, Brahms, Tschaikowsky, Wolf and Strauss. Her insistence that an operatic artist should be a musician as well as a singer was unique, and her practice created a standard. Her programs explored the song literature of all ages and all peoples. Her mastery of style enabled her to sing with equal authority, music of Bach and Beethoven, as well as Debussy and Ravel.

Beginning her Concert years in America

Her folksong recital, in which she sang the songs of more than a dozen countries in the language native to each, was described by one eminent critic as "epoch-making". Up to this time her work in America had been entirely devoted to opera. The succeeding years which included as well her song recitals, marked the beginning of her greatest period of contribution to the development of music in America.

As Henderson wrote:

> "The singer who drew the vocal line of Violetta with such perfection, who vitalized every phrase of Lucia and who bubbled over with the comedy of Rosina, was the same artist who drew the vocal line of scores of songs as no one else has drawn them. Whatever the power was that guided her, — dramatic instinct, pure musical genius or a deep and subtle womanhood, which is not for a mere commentator to estimate — she was an artist unique and supreme."

Her superiority as a singer of lieder was recognized by the eminent musical figures of her day. Clara Schumann, the composer's devoted widow, invariably urged her to "Sing Robert's songs for the world" (and Robert had written most of them for Clara herself, just before their marriage).

Sembrich's friendship with Brahms lasted to the end of his life, for he, like other great musicians of his time, recognized the young singer's interpretative genius. In response to her question concerning the rendering of one or another of his songs, he is known to have replied: "I trust you perfectly to interpret my intention in what you feel inspired to do." Referring to her faculty of imaginative re-creating, he further said: "Sembrich has a mind — a heart, and a soul."

"Quite apart from other considerations, of technic, training, experience — Sembrich had in her singing a kind of feeling that went right to the heart."

This singer who so prodigiously marked the development of American concert life was the same artist and the same woman who had brought a sovereign persuasiveness into the portrayal of her operatic roles.

Heylbut and Gerber wrote of her in opera:

"Sembrich's assumption of young roles carried convincing illusion. . . . Her flawless taste in costuming, her fine care for the detail of her appearance, and the sheer zeal of purpose that animated her, caused her not to represent, but to *become*, the part she sang. And a houseful of spectators watched her become the part and believed it."

Marcella Sembrich and Lilli Lehmann held commanding positions among immortal interpreters of song as well as of opera. Sembrich was fortunate in the length of her career, for it permitted her to realize the full depth of her artistry in every field; yet this very length was the token of her personal attributes, her health and vitality, the perduring correctness of her workmanship, the animation and breadth of her spirit, the inexhaustible wealth of her interest and the innate radiancy of her intellect. Consummate, sovereign and unspoiled, she had a unique suppleness of temperament, something of the abiding firmness of the peasant, a patrician sense of fitness and the eloquence of the true artist. With unclouded ideals from which she never swerved, she had also a *force of intention* that placed her in a class apart that enabled her to mark as her own, the era in which she sang and which gave her name its singular halo.

A RECOLLECTION OF MARCELLA SEMBRICH

Behind her greatness as an artist the public instinctively sensed Sembrich's greatness as a woman and came to perceive, too, her unstinted dedication of herself to the cause of music. The first time a New York audience ever rose in tribute to an artist coming on the concert stage, was at a Sembrich recital at Carnegie Hall. Some of us can recall that Isadore Luckstone and Rubin Goldmark were among her accompanists. However, throughout many years of concert tours her colleague at the piano was the young, outstandingly gifted Frank La Forge.

Sembrich's inborn kindness to fellow-artists was legendary, and she gave benefit performances in America and in Europe with a boundless generosity for which she was universally beloved. One of these performances occurred upon the return of the Metropolitan Company from the horrors of the San Francisco fire of April 1906. It is of interest to read Krehbiel's comment:

> "The Opera Company was overwhelmed by the catastrophe of the earthquake which sent it back a physical and financial wreck. The calamity tested the fortitude and the philosophy of Mr. Grau, as well as the artists, but through the gloom there shone a cheering ray when Madame Sembrich, herself one of the chief sufferers from the earthquake, postponed her return to her European home long enough to give a concert at Carnegie Hall for minor members of the Company, distributing more than $10,000 to musicians whose instrument had been lost in San Francisco."

Soon afterward Madame Sembrich and her husband sailed for Europe, returning to their home in Switzerland.

In the hospitable de Coppet Villa on Lake Geneva — August 1912

Standing: Mrs. Edward J. de Coppet and Ernest Schelling
Seated: Madame Sembrich, and at her feet, Edward J. de Coppet
To the Right: Ignace Paderewski and Mme. Paderewska
Directly Above: Sigismond Stojowski

Through the years it was an established custom with Madame Sembrich to "set aside several weeks each summer for mountain climbing, her favorite pastime. During these Alpine tours she stored away tremendous vitality."

Vacationing in Switzerland

Mme. Sembrich at the base of the Matterhorn near Zermatt.

"Silent and lofty altitudes gave her a feeling of expansion where her spirit felt alone and free."

Following the final European tour of 1909-10 that brought her operatic career to a close, Sembrich moved to Nice, with the hope that the southern climate would be beneficial to her husband. However, with the outbreak of World War I in 1914, they bade farewell to the French Riviera and sailed from Holland back to America.

Goodbye to the Riviera — 1914

They made their winter home in New York, while their summers were spent at Lake Placid up to the time of Professor Stengel's death. When Madame Sembrich was left a widow in 1917, she withdrew completely from public life, and with her husband no longer at her side, she decided in 1921 to make her summer home on the shores of Lake George.

Upon her retirement, however, she was not content to cease her activities, and like some of her celebrated predecessors, Garcia, Malibran and Marchesi, she turned to the profession of teaching, and accepted Directorship of the Vocal Departments of Curtis Institute of Music in Philadelphia and Juilliard Graduate School in New York City.

From 1918 up to the time of her death in 1935, Madame Sembrich remained a living link with the age of great singing, devoting herself to passing on inspiring interpretations to a younger generation. Her position in the world of music resembled that of Liszt in the Weimar days, for to her home on Lake George came artists of all nationalities, seeking guidance in the art in which, in her own words, "she had learned so thoroughly and practiced so long". To each she gave freely of the riches of her long experience. Her keen understanding and profound honesty were as inspiring as her magnificent technique and incomparable art. It was amazing to see her piano stacked with modern compositions, for which her interest was always alive. She actively encouraged the founding of opera companies in American cities and kept in closest touch with contemporary musical activity.

THE de COPPET MUSIC ROOM IN NEW YORK WAS A RENDEZVOUS WHERE NOT ONLY ARTISTS OF RENOWN, BUT COUNTLESS MUSIC LOVERS GATHERED THROUGH THE YEARS

FRONT ROW – Alma Gluck, Guillaume Stengel, Mrs. Kreisler, Efrem Zimbalist, Pablo Casals, Susan Metcalf (Mme. Casals), Katherine Goodson (Mrs. Hinton), Mme. Hélène Paderewska

MIDDLE ROW – Adolfo Betti, Ossip Gabrilowitsch, Edward J. de Coppet, Fritz Kreisler, Mme. Sembrich, Clara Clemens (Mme. Gabrilowitsch), Ignace Paderewski, Mrs. E. J. de Coppet and Daughter

STANDING – Ugo Ara, Ivan d'Archambeau, Arthur Hinton, André de Coppet, Alfred Pochon, Sigismond Stojowski, Rudolf Ganz

New York – 1916

The Maples Cottage, Lake Placid, New York
"Reflecting upon the future of her young protegées"
about 1919

* * * Without discouraging gifted young aspirants, it is wise to encourage a deeper realization of the step they are taking in a long pilgrimage that demands sacrifice, untiring energy and humility."

"Few will realize how much hardship, discipline and self-denial I had undergone, struggling with poverty that hampered me throughout my years of study.

Photograph taken in September 1934

INTERIOR OF THE MARCELLA SEMBRICH STUDIO AT BOLTON, LAKE GEORGE.

The Studio at Bolton on Lake George, built by her in 1924, has been converted into a memorial to one whom critics hailed as immortal. It was opened to the public during July and August 1937, and ever since has become a summer pilgrimage point for thousands of visitors. Maintained as when she was there, this simple memorial, with the affection and admiration of the great public, is now preserved by the Marcella Sembrich Memorial Association, Inc.

In the words of a great dramatic writer comes this tribute:

> "Of her more than three score and ten years, it might be said —'they were the lifetime of a soul that never lost its honor and a spirit that never lost its eagerness.'"

The Studio — an unpretentious stucco building stands beneath immense
pines on the Sembrich Point at Bolton-on-Lake George, New York

Here in the woods where Silence reigns
  More eloquent than Sound,
The place I stand on 'neath the trees
  Seems somehow, holy ground.

The birds withhold their carolling
  The breeze abandons play:
And Heaven in this atmosphere
  Seems not so far away!

Martha Martin

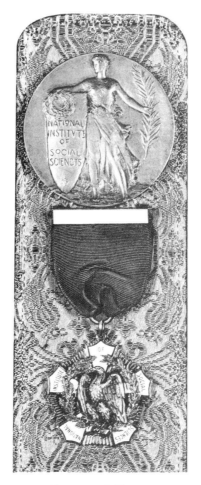

Badge and Medal
designed by Malvina Hofmann and
presented to Madame Sembrich in 1930
by The Institute of Social Sciences
"For distinguished Service to Humanity"